THE CUBE
FOR CHILDREN

JESSICA ZOUTSOS

ERNO'S CUBE LTD

First published by Erno's Cube™ Limited in 2023

ISBN 9781399965446

FOREWORD

Invented by Ernő Rubik in 1974, the cube has gained worldwide fame for its staggering complexity. With a mind-boggling 43 quintillion possible patterns, there's no wonder it's considered one of the most challenging puzzles ever created.

This mysterious cube soon became known as the Magic Cube – surely you would need magical powers to solve it?

In fact, solving this seemingly impossible puzzle is not beyond your reach.

Within these pages, we will guide you through the step-by-step process of solving the cube, with each step requiring concentration, problem solving and memory to complete.

But our adventure doesn't stop there. Once you've grasped the method, we'll take you on a journey towards memorisation, so you can dazzle your friends and family with your newfound cube-solving skills.

Psst...I'll let you in on a secret - some grown-ups don't know how to solve the cube either, so you might want to let them borrow this book!

For Edward and Harriet

With thanks to Lisa Jo Robinson
and Della Oliver

CONTENTS

PART 1

GETTING TO KNOW YOUR CUBE

First, we will explain the different pieces that make up the cube and show you how to move them around

PART 2

LEARNING THE METHOD

Through 7 chapters, we will work through the step-by-step process of solving the cube. At the end of this part, you will have solved the cube!

PART 3

MEMORISING THE METHOD

Next, we will guide you through a story that threads together each step so that you can memorise the method

PART 4

PRACTISING THE SEQUENCES

Finally, we will focus solely on practising the sequences used to solve the cube so that you can develop "muscle memory"

PART 1

GETTING TO KNOW
YOUR CUBE

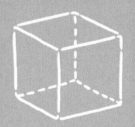

The cube has **6** faces...

When the cube is
solved, each face
is just **ONE**
colour

WHITE

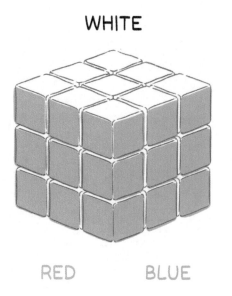

RED   BLUE

YELLOW

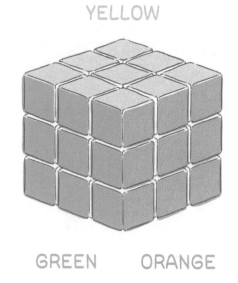

GREEN   ORANGE

It is made of **26** pieces...

Each **PIECE**
of the cube is
UNIQUE

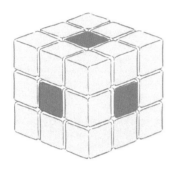

CENTRE pieces have **1** colour

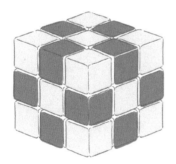

EDGE pieces have **2** colours

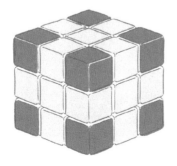

CORNER pieces have **3** colours

The colour of the **CENTRE** piece is the colour that face will be when the cube is **SOLVED**

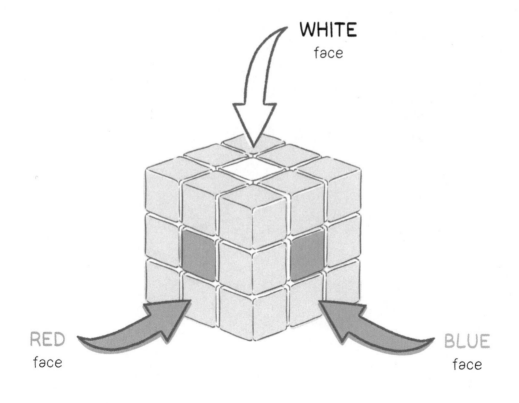

WHITE face

RED face

BLUE face

 LEFT

 RIGHT

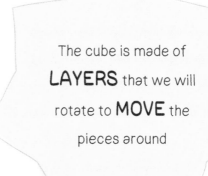

The cube is made of **LAYERS** that we will rotate to **MOVE** the pieces around

 TOP

 BOTTOM

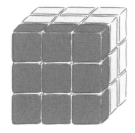 FRONT

Let's learn some **MOVES**...

Rotate the **LEFT** layer

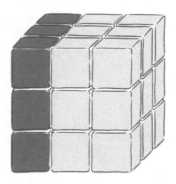

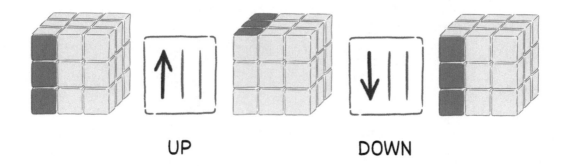

UP   DOWN

Rotate the **RIGHT** layer

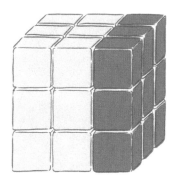

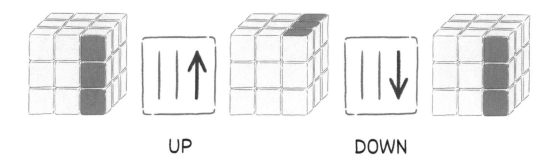

UP   DOWN

Rotate the **TOP** layer

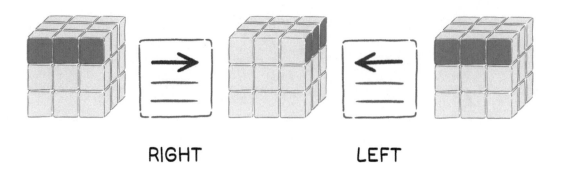

RIGHT   LEFT

Rotate the **BOTTOM** layer

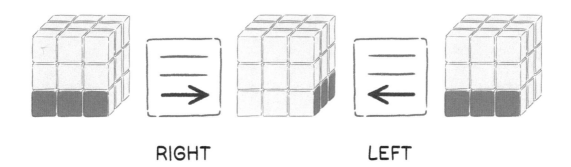

RIGHT   LEFT

Rotate the **FRONT** layer

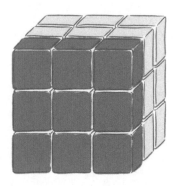

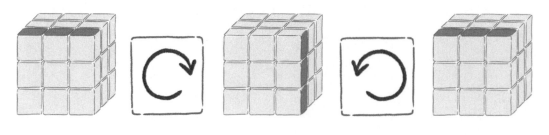

CLOCKWISE   ANTI-CLOCKWISE

Well done! You now know the **10 MOVES** needed to solve the cube.

Keep practising...

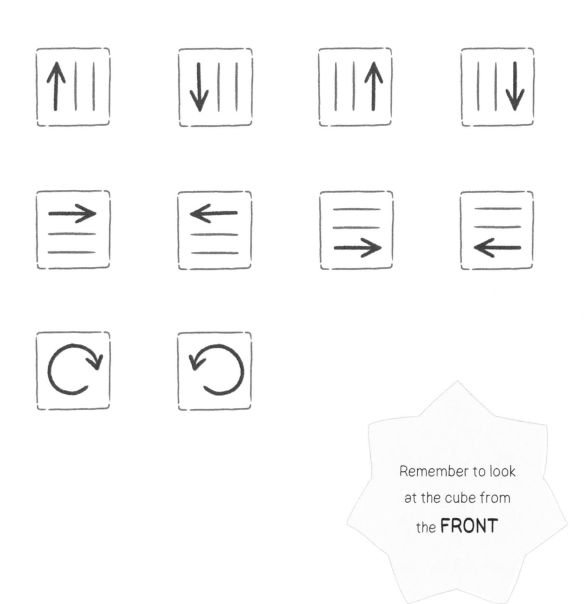

Remember to look at the cube from the **FRONT**

16

A **SEQUENCE** is a series of **MOVES**.

Give this one a try:

Remember to look at the cube from the **FRONT** and try to hold the cube **STILL**

When you start a sequence, try to remember the

COLOUR of the **CENTRE** piece that is facing you.

This will **STAY THE SAME** during the sequence.

Is it RED, BLUE, GREEN or ORANGE?

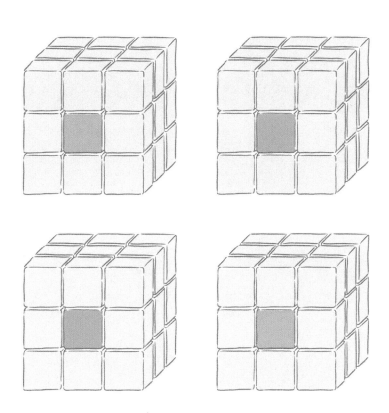

PART 2

LEARNING THE
METHOD

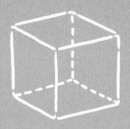

We will solve the cube one **LAYER** at a time...

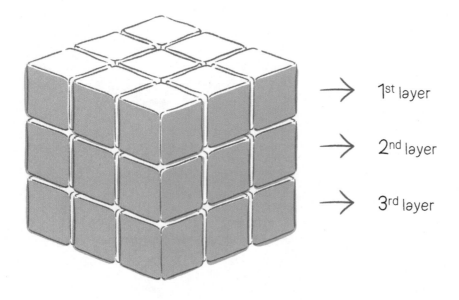

$\longrightarrow$ 1st layer

$\longrightarrow$ 2nd layer

$\longrightarrow$ 3rd layer

...through **SEVEN** chapters:

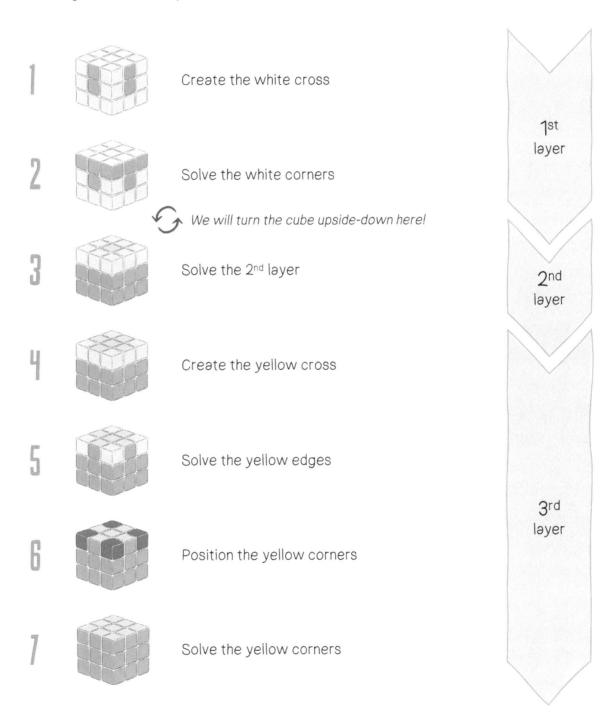

1   Create the white cross

2   Solve the white corners

    We will turn the cube upside-down here!

3   Solve the 2nd layer

4   Create the yellow cross

5   Solve the yellow edges

6   Position the yellow corners

7   Solve the yellow corners

1st layer

2nd layer

3rd layer

22

Remember, the cube is meant to be challenging
so it's okay to make mistakes.

Try one chapter at a time. If you make a mistake,
go back to Chapter 1 and try again.

Whenever you see this symbol,
read the note in the red box!

CHAPTER 1

CREATE THE WHITE
CROSS

SUMMARY OF CHAPTER 1

In this chapter we will create a **WHITE CROSS** with colourful legs, by solving these **WHITE EDGE** pieces:

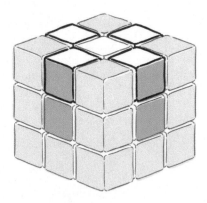

Find the **WHITE** centre piece and keep this facing **UPWARDS** for this chapter.

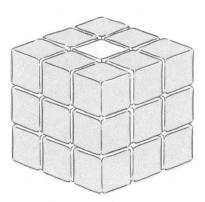

STEP 1

Look in the **BOTTOM** layer for an
EDGE piece with **WHITE** on it...

WHITE
+
ANY COLOUR

Found one?

Lucky you!

Skip to STEP ③

There aren't any!

Don't worry...
Look for one in the
TOP or **MIDDLE** layer

Go to STEP ②

STEP 2

We need to move your piece to the **BOTTOM** layer.

Which layer is your piece in?

TOP

Hold your cube like this:

Do these **MOVES**

MIDDLE

Hold your cube like this:

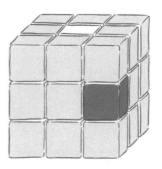

Do this **MOVE**

Go to STEP 3

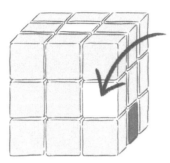

If you have **WHITE** here after this move, you might have broken one of the legs of your white cross...

Don't worry, you can fix it by doing this:

This moves your edge piece out of the way and then fixes the broken leg of the white cross

Now find your edge piece in the **BOTTOM** layer and go to STEP

STEP 3

Which colour did you find?

White and ... ?

ROTATE the **BOTTOM** layer to move your piece to the face with the **SAME COLOUR** in the **CENTRE**. Your cube will look like one of these:

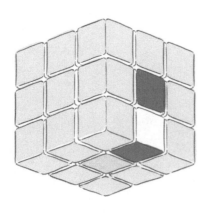

OR

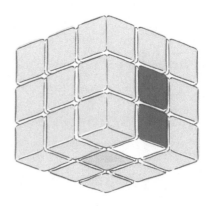

For example, if your piece is white and BLUE:

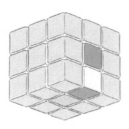

OR

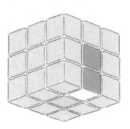

Well done! Go to STEP

STEP 4

Now we will move your piece up to the **TOP** layer.

Hold your cube like this:

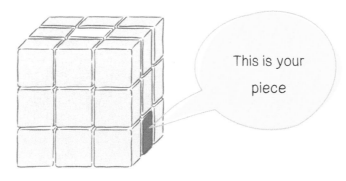

This is your piece

Do these **MOVES**:

Which one do you have?

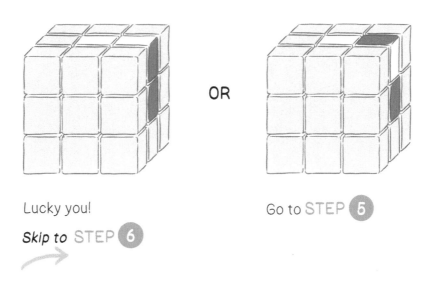

Lucky you!

Skip to STEP 6

Go to STEP 5

STEP 5

Hold your cube like this:

Do this **SEQUENCE**:

Now your cube looks like this:

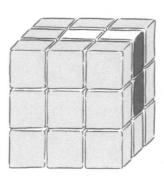

STEP 6

Well done! You've solved part of the white cross.

Go back to STEP **1** and **REPEAT** these steps until **ALL 4 LEGS** are solved and you can see the **WHITE CROSS**, like this:

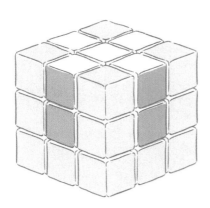 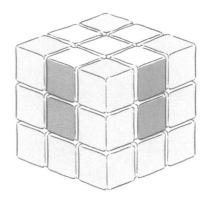

Well done,

you've completed Chapter 1!

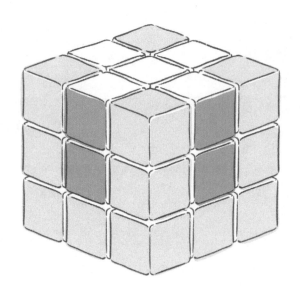

CHAPTER 2

SOLVE THE
WHITE CORNERS

SUMMARY OF CHAPTER 2

In this chapter we will solve the **4 WHITE CORNER** pieces to complete the white face, like this...

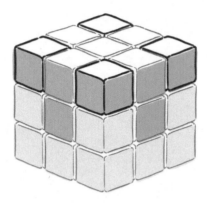

Keep the **WHITE** face facing **UPWARDS** for this chapter.

STEP 1

Look in the **BOTTOM** layer for a
CORNER piece with **WHITE** on it...

WHITE
+
2 COLOURS

Found one?

Lucky you!

Skip to STEP ❸

There aren't any!

Look for one in the
TOP layer

Go to STEP ❷

STEP 2

We need to move your piece to the **BOTTOM** layer.

Hold your cube like this:

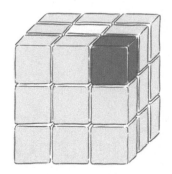

Do this **SEQUENCE**:

Go to STEP 3

STEP 3

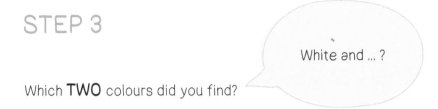

Which **TWO** colours did you find?

White and ... ?

ROTATE the **BOTTOM** layer to move your piece so that it sits between the faces that **MATCH** these **COLOURS**.

For example, if you have white, RED and BLUE:

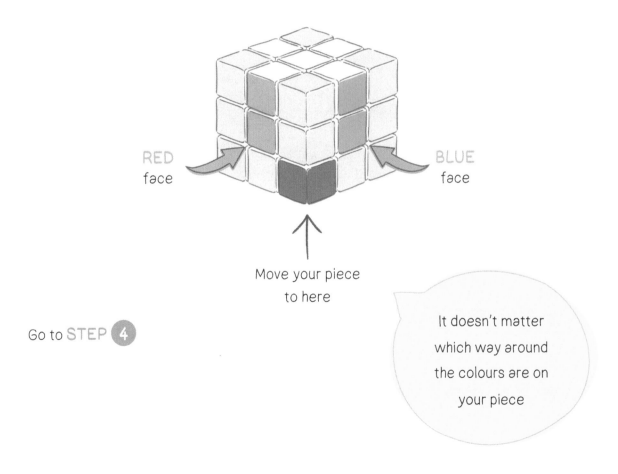

RED face

BLUE face

Move your piece to here

It doesn't matter which way around the colours are on your piece

Go to STEP ④

STEP 4

Hold your cube like this:

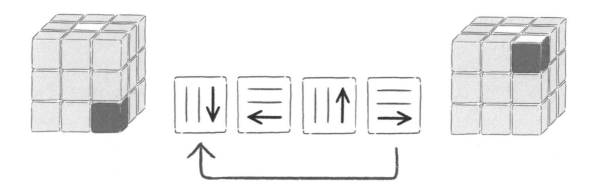

REPEAT this sequence until
your piece is in the **TOP** corner
and is **SOLVED**, with white
facing upwards

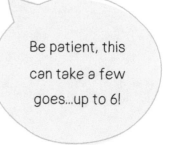

Be patient, this
can take a few
goes...up to 6!

STEP 5

Well done! You've solved a white corner.

Go back to STEP ❶ and **REPEAT** these steps until **ALL 4 CORNERS** are solved and your cube looks like this:

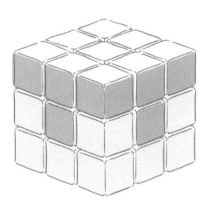 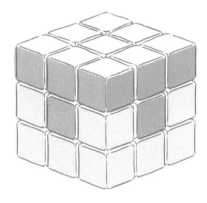

Well done, you've completed

Chapter 2 and solved the 1st layer!

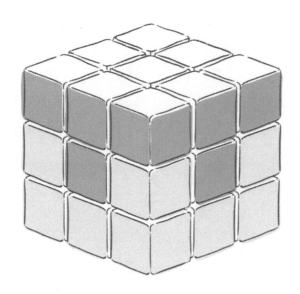

CHAPTER 3

SOLVE THE
2nd LAYER

SUMMARY OF CHAPTER 3

In this chapter we will solve these **4 EDGE** pieces:

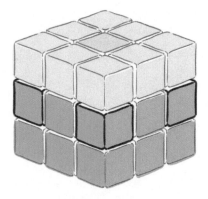

Turn the cube **UPSIDE-DOWN** from now on, so the YELLOW centre piece is

facing **UPWARDS**.

STEP 1

Look in the **TOP** layer for an **EDGE** piece...

> Any **2 COLOURS**,
> but **NOT** YELLOW

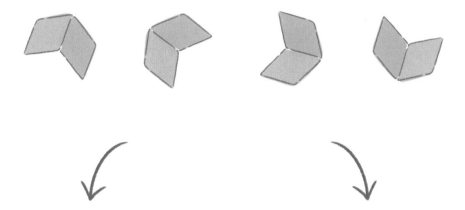

Found one?

Lucky you!

Skip to STEP **3**

There aren't any!

Look for one in the
MIDDLE layer, that is not
already solved

Go to STEP **2**

STEP 2

We need to move your piece to the **TOP** layer.

Hold your cube like this:

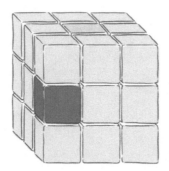

Do this **SEQUENCE**:

Well done! Find your piece in the **TOP** layer and go to STEP

STEP 3

Which colour do you have here on your piece?

ROTATE the **TOP** layer to make an **UPSIDE-DOWN T** of the **SAME COLOUR**, like this...

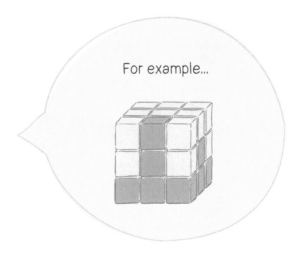

For example...

STEP 4

Which colour is on the **TOP** of your piece?

Should this colour move down to the **LEFT** or down to the **RIGHT**?

For example, a BLUE T with a RED TOP:

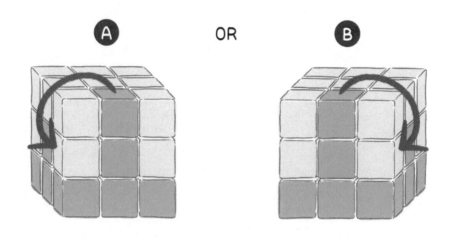

Solve your piece using **SEQUENCE** A or B

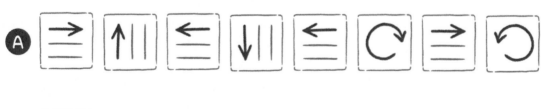

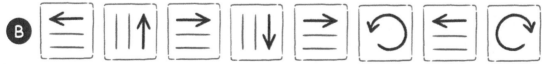

STEP 5

Well done! You've solved part of the 2nd layer.

Go back to STEP 1 and **REPEAT** these steps until **ALL 4 PIECES** are solved and your cube looks like this:

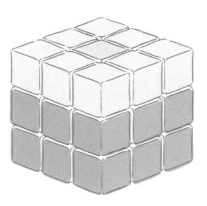 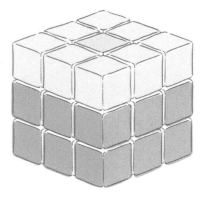

Well done, you've completed

Chapter 3 and solved the 2nd layer!

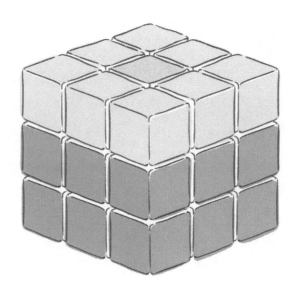

CHAPTER 4

CREATE THE
YELLOW CROSS

SUMMARY OF CHAPTER 4

In this chapter we will make a YELLOW CROSS on top of the cube, like this:

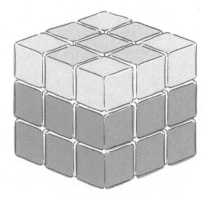

Keep the YELLOW face facing **UPWARDS** for this chapter.

STEP 1

Look for one of these **PATTERNS** on the yellow face:

OR OR

Found one?

Well done! Go to STEP 2

You may also have yellow on the other pieces - you can ignore these

If you already have a yellow cross, you can skip this chapter and go to Chapter 5!

STEP 2

The **SEQUENCE** below turns each pattern into the next one along until finally the
YELLOW CROSS:

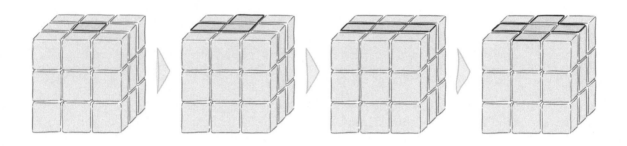

Hold your cube like one of the cubes above.

REPEAT this sequence until you have the
YELLOW CROSS:

Make sure you hold
your cube like one of
the cubes above
before you repeat
the sequence

Now your cube looks like this:

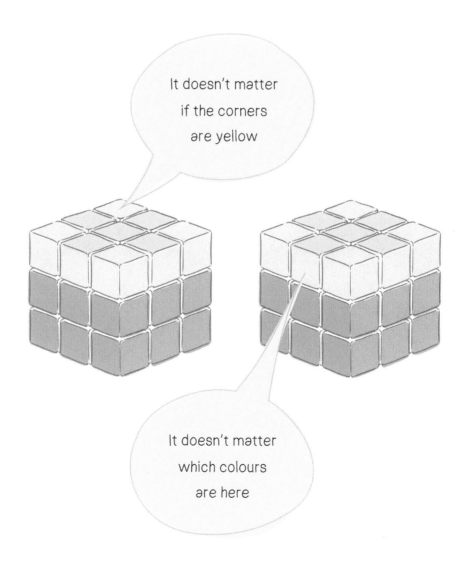

It doesn't matter if the corners are yellow

It doesn't matter which colours are here

Well done,

you've completed Chapter 4!

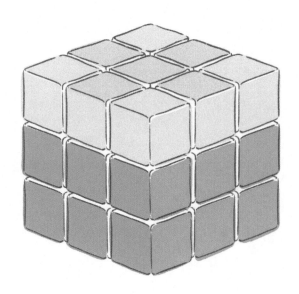

CHAPTER 5

SOLVE THE
YELLOW EDGES

SUMMARY OF CHAPTER 5

In this chapter we will match the **LEGS** of the YELLOW CROSS with the blue, red, green and orange faces...

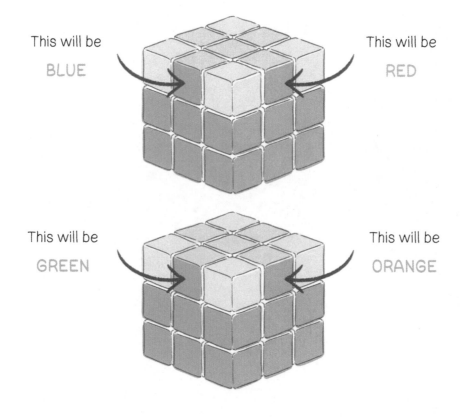

This will be BLUE

This will be RED

This will be GREEN

This will be ORANGE

If the colours of the legs already match, you can skip to Chapter 6!

STEP 1

ROTATE the yellow cross into each of its **4** possible positions to find one where...

2 ADJACENT LEGS are **CORRECT**

ADJACENT means...

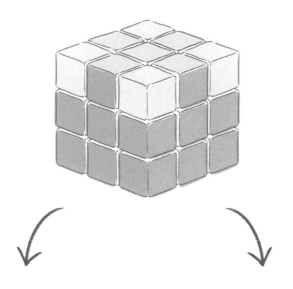

For example...

Done it? Well done!

Skip to STEP **3**

It's not possible!

No problem...

Go to STEP **2**

STEP 2

Hold your cube like this:

Do this **SEQUENCE**:

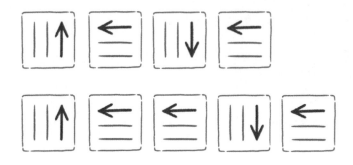

Go **BACK** to STEP 1

STEP 3

Turn your cube around and look at the **OTHER 2 LEGS**...

They need to **SWAP** places!

Hold your cube like this:

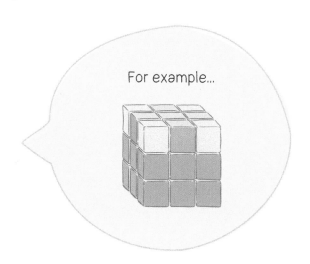

For example...

Do this **SEQUENCE** to swap them around:

 If they are also correct, you can skip to Chapter 6!

Well done,

you've completed Chapter 5!

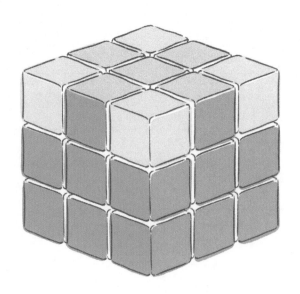

CHAPTER 6

POSITION THE
YELLOW CORNERS

SUMMARY OF CHAPTER 6

In this chapter we will move the 4 YELLOW CORNER pieces to the correct corners of the cube...

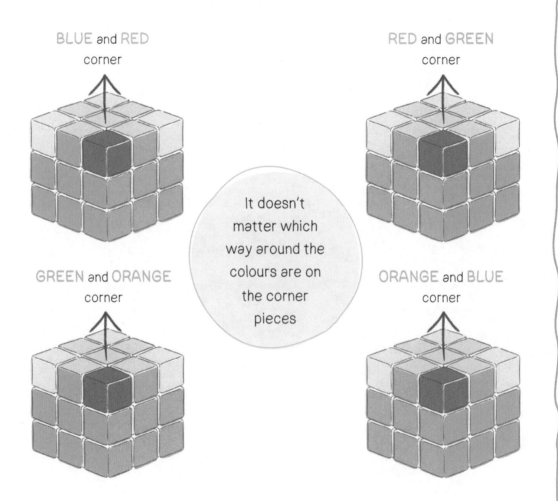

BLUE and RED
corner

RED and GREEN
corner

It doesn't matter which way around the colours are on the corner pieces

GREEN and ORANGE
corner

ORANGE and BLUE
corner

If all 4 corner pieces are already in the correct place, you can skip to Chapter 7!

STEP 1

Look at the **CORNER** pieces in the **TOP** layer.

Try to find a corner piece that is in the **CORRECT** place - between the faces with **MATCHING COLOURS**.

For example...

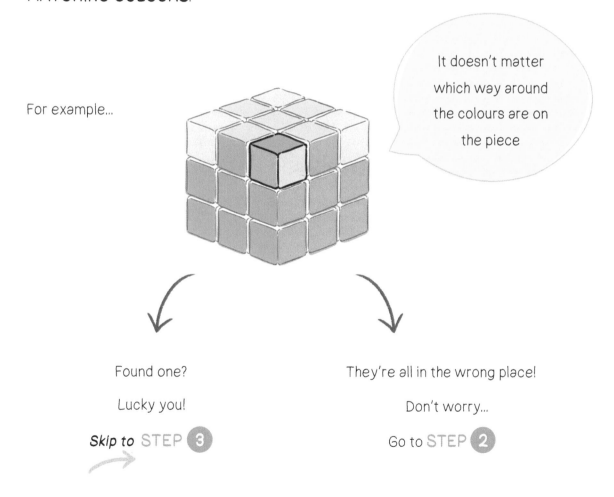

It doesn't matter which way around the colours are on the piece

Found one?

Lucky you!

Skip to STEP **3**

They're all in the wrong place!

Don't worry...

Go to STEP **2**

STEP 2

Hold your cube like this:

Do this **SEQUENCE**:

Go **BACK** to STEP

STEP 3

Hold your cube like this:

This is the **CORRECT** piece

REPEAT this sequence until **ALL 4** corners are positioned between the faces with **MATCHING COLOURS**:

Remember, it doesn't matter which way around the colours are on the corner pieces

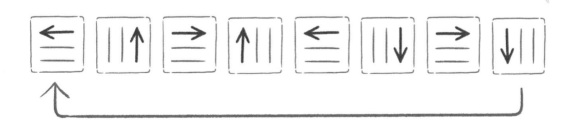

Well done,

you've completed Chapter 6!

ORANGE and GREEN
corner

BLUE and ORANGE
corner

GREEN and RED
corner

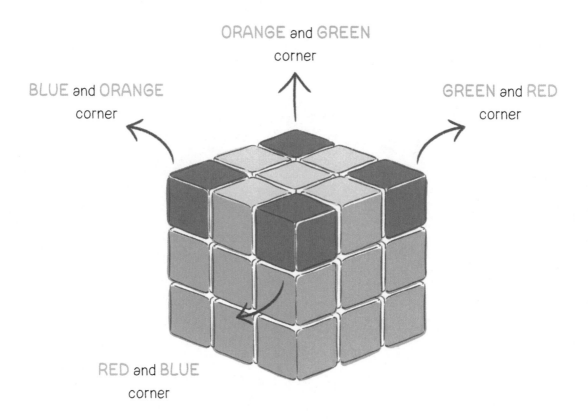

RED and BLUE
corner

CHAPTER 7

SOLVE THE
YELLOW CORNERS

SUMMARY OF CHAPTER 7

In this final chapter we will **SOLVE THE CUBE** by turning the YELLOW

CORNER pieces around so that yellow is facing upwards.

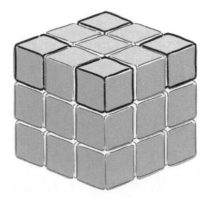

Keep the YELLOW face facing **UPWARDS** for this chapter.

STEP 1

Find a **CORNER** that we need to solve - where yellow is **NOT** facing upwards, like this one...

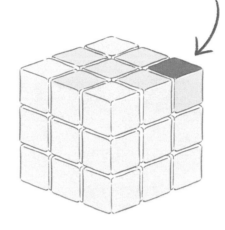

Hold your cube like this:

Which colour do you have in the centre? For this chapter, we will call this your

FAVOURITE 🖤 colour.

Remember this colour - it will stay the same until you solve the cube!

STEP 2

Do this **SEQUENCE**:

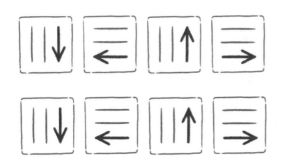

This sequence will
MIX UP
the other pieces of the cube.
Don't worry, they will go back
to their correct places as we
go through this chapter

Is YELLOW facing upwards?

NO	YES
REPEAT	Go to
the sequence	STEP ③

STEP 3

Look for another corner we need to solve, where yellow is **NOT** facing upwards.

Keep your **FAVOURITE**  colour facing you.

ROTATE the **TOP** layer to bring the corner into this position:

Go **BACK** to STEP 2

When **ALL 4 CORNERS** have YELLOW facing upwards, go to STEP 4

STEP 4

ROTATE the **TOP** layer to **SOLVE** the cube.

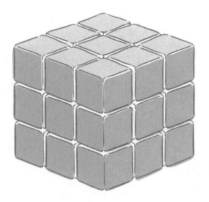 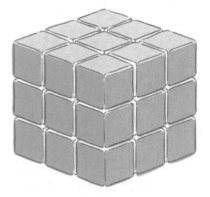

HOORAY!

Great job,

you've solved the cube!

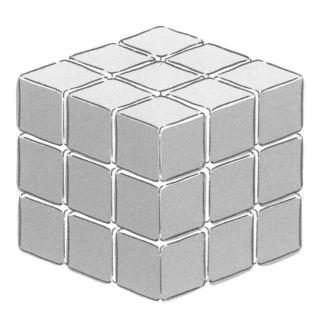

PART 3

MEMORISING THE METHOD

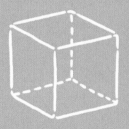

Now that you have mastered the method, your
next challenge is to memorise it.

In this part, we will solve the cube using the same
method we have just used in Part 2, but with a story that
takes you on a journey through each chapter.

This time, we won't give you as many instructions, but
don't worry, if you get stuck, you can always go back to
the same chapter in Part 2 for some extra help.

This part will help you to remember each step and each
sequence. Visualising the story will help you to solve the
cube without opening this book!

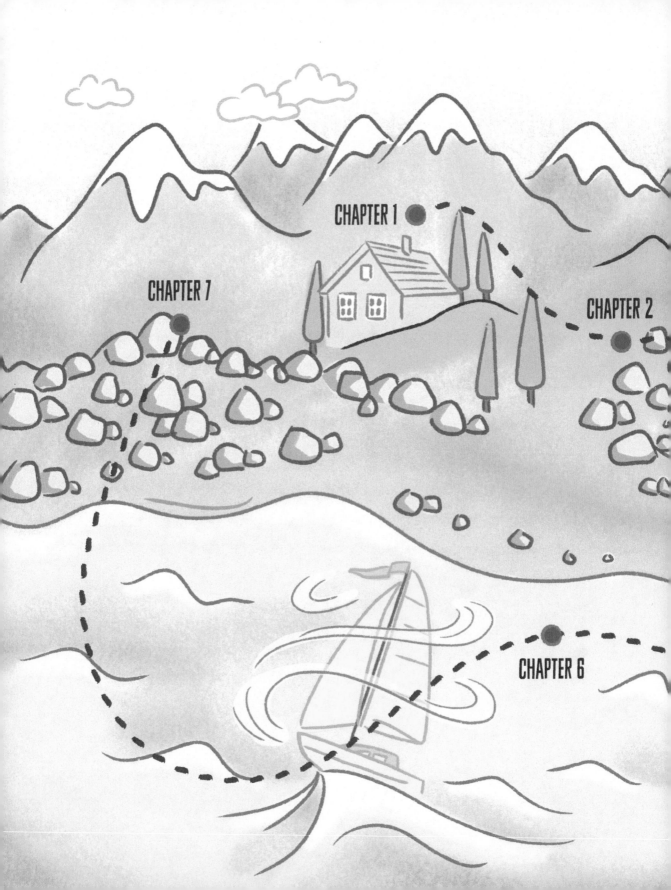

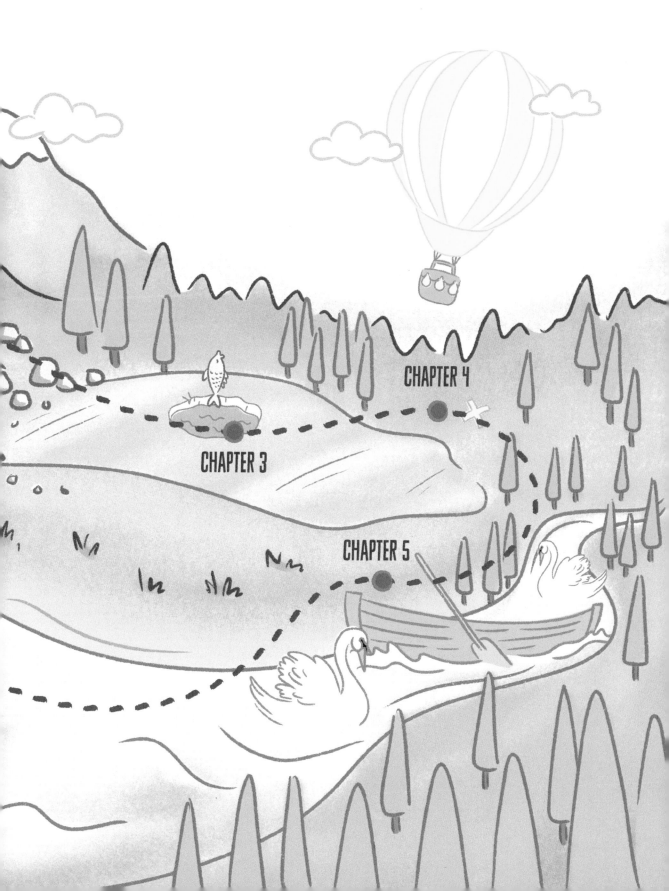

You live in a house in the mountains. While going for a walk you come across a treasure map...

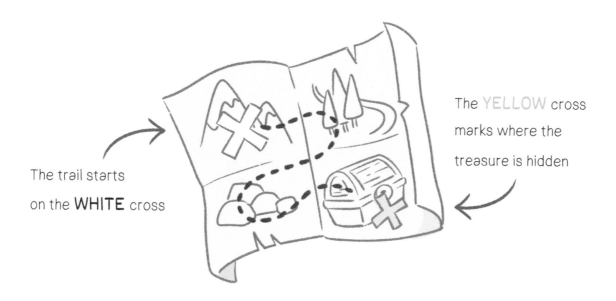

The trail starts
on the **WHITE** cross

The YELLOW cross
marks where the
treasure is hidden

Solving the cube will take you on a journey to find the treasure and bring it home!

CHAPTER 1

Your first task is to find the **WHITE CROSS!**

Keep the **WHITE** centre piece facing **UPWARDS**.

Look in the **BOTTOM** layer for one of these...

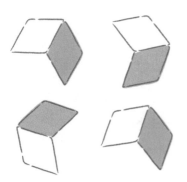

If there aren't any, find one in the

TOP or **MIDDLE**

layer and move it to the bottom layer

Which colour did you find? **ROTATE** the **BOTTOM** layer to move your piece to the face with the **SAME COLOUR** in the **CENTRE**.

Now move your piece up to the **TOP** layer:

If the colours are the **WRONG WAY** around, fix them with this sequence:

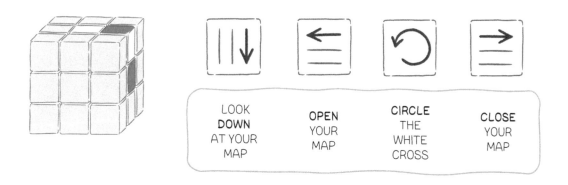

LOOK **DOWN** AT YOUR MAP	**OPEN** YOUR MAP	**CIRCLE** THE WHITE CROSS	**CLOSE** YOUR MAP

REPEAT these steps until **ALL 4 LEGS** are solved and you can see the **WHITE CROSS**.

Now your cube looks like this:

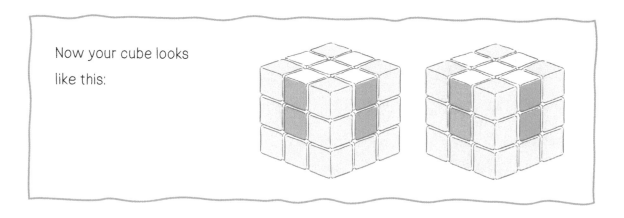

CHAPTER 2

You set off down the mountain with the map and make your way through a boulder field.

Look in the **BOTTOM** layer for one of these frosty white boulders...

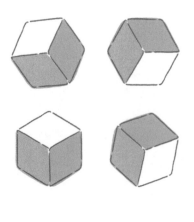

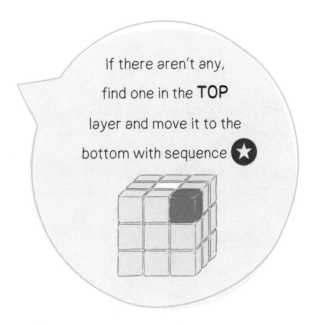

If there aren't any, find one in the **TOP** layer and move it to the bottom with sequence ⭐

Which **TWO** colours did you find? **ROTATE** the **BOTTOM** layer to move your piece so that it sits between the faces that **MATCH** these **COLOURS**.

REPEAT the sequence below until your piece

is in the **TOP** corner and is **SOLVED**...

Remember, this can take a few goes!

As you clamber over the boulders, you go...

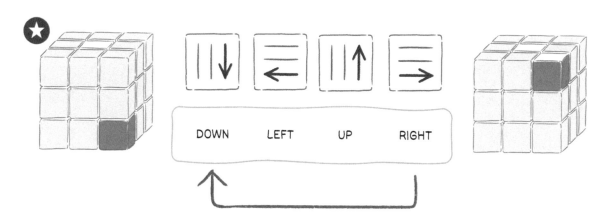

DOWN   LEFT   UP   RIGHT

REPEAT these steps until **ALL 4 CORNERS** are solved.

Now your cube looks like this:

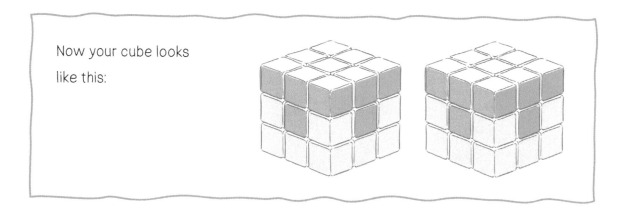

CHAPTER 3

 Turn your cube upside-down so YELLOW is facing upwards.

You reach the end of the boulder field and come across a frozen lake. You're feeling hungry after all that climbing, so you make a hole in the ice and try to catch a fish. Your first task is to make a **FISHING HOOK**.

Look in the **TOP** layer for one of these...

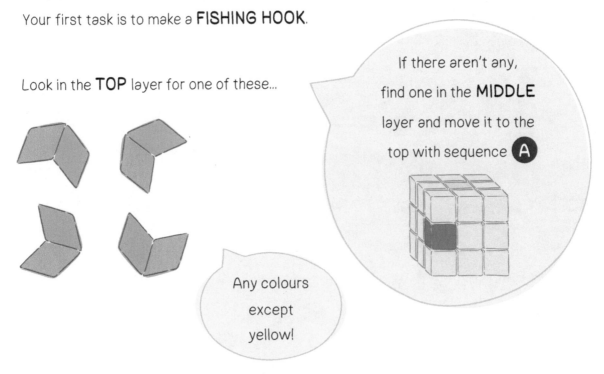

If there aren't any, find one in the **MIDDLE** layer and move it to the top with sequence (A)

Any colours except yellow!

Which colour is on the **SIDE** of your piece? **ROTATE** the **TOP** layer to make a **FISHING HOOK** (an upside-down T) of the **SAME COLOUR**.

Which colour is on the **TOP** of your piece? Should this colour move down to the left or down to the right? For example, a RED TOP:

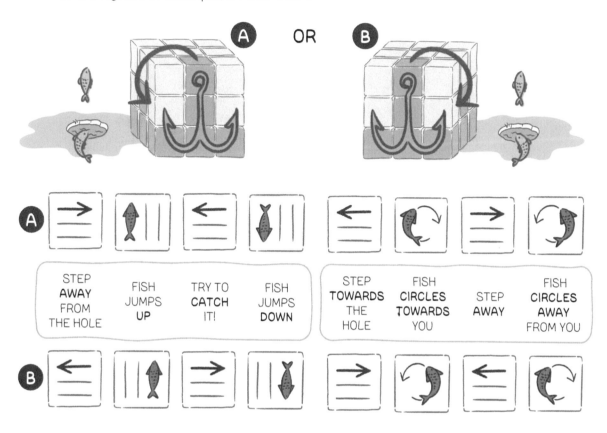

REPEAT these steps until **ALL 4 PIECES** are solved.

Now your cube looks like this:

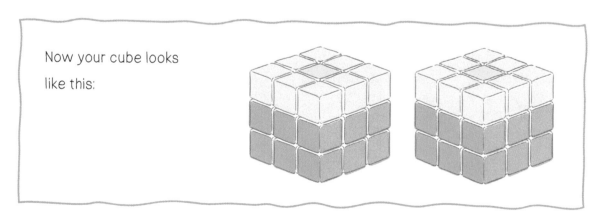

CHAPTER 4

You reach the edge of the frozen lake and find a
hot air balloon tethered to the ground.

Can you use the balloon to spot the YELLOW CROSS and find the treasure?

Look for one of these patterns on the yellow face:

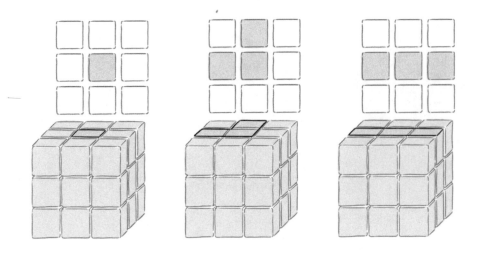

Hold your cube like one of the cubes above.

Now do this
sequence:

| ROLL INTO THE BALLOON | FLOAT UP | HEAD WIND | FLOAT DOWN | TAIL WIND | ROLL OUT OF THE BALLOON |

Did you find the YELLOW CROSS?

NO

Climb back into the balloon
and try the sequence again.

YES

Well done!
You have found the

Now your cube looks
like this:

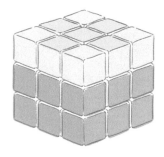 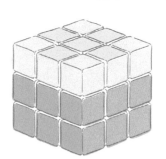

CHAPTER 5

It's time to go home.

The treasure is too heavy to carry all the way home, so you take a rowing boat down the river.

ROTATE the yellow cross into each of its **4** possible positions to find one where **2 ADJACENT LEGS** are **CORRECT**.

Like this...

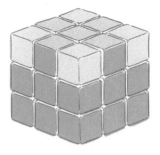

If this is not possible, do sequence ⭐ and try again!

Turn your cube around and look at the **OTHER 2 LEGS** – if they need to **SWAP**, do this sequence:

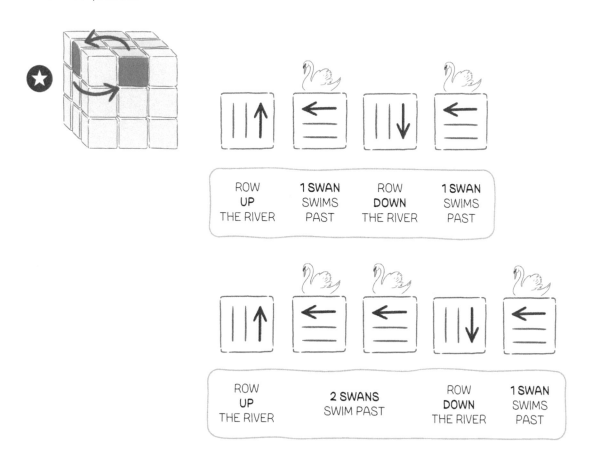

⭐

| ROW UP THE RIVER | 1 SWAN SWIMS PAST | ROW DOWN THE RIVER | 1 SWAN SWIMS PAST |

| ROW UP THE RIVER | 2 SWANS SWIM PAST | ROW DOWN THE RIVER | 1 SWAN SWIMS PAST |

Now your cube looks like this:

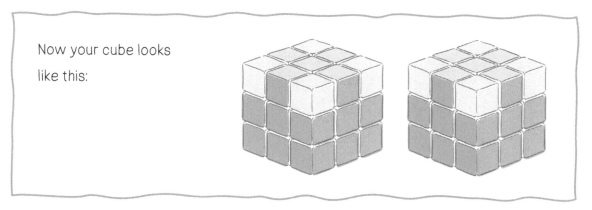

CHAPTER 6

Finally, the river reaches the sea.

There is a storm coming - you will need a bigger boat, so you swap your rowing boat for a sailing boat and sail out into the waves.

Look at the **CORNER** pieces in the **TOP** layer. Find one that is in the **CORRECT** place - between the faces with **MATCHING COLOURS**, like this...

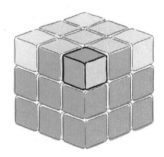

It doesn't matter which way around the colours are on the piece

If all 4 corners are in the wrong place, do sequence ⭐ and have another look

REPEAT this sequence until **ALL 4** corners are positioned between the faces with **MATCHING COLOURS**:

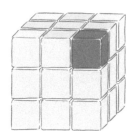

> Remember, it doesn't matter which way around the colours are on the corner pieces

⭐

| WIND FROM THE **FRONT** | SAILS **UP** AT THE FRONT | WIND FROM THE **BACK** | SAILS **UP** AT THE BACK | | WIND FROM THE **FRONT** | SAILS **DOWN** AT THE FRONT | WIND FROM THE **BACK** | SAILS **DOWN** AT THE BACK |

Now your cube looks like this:

ORANGE and GREEN corner

BLUE and ORANGE corner

GREEN and RED corner

RED and BLUE corner

CHAPTER 7

You make it to shore at the foot of the mountain where you live.

Look for a **CORNER** piece where the yellow side is **NOT** facing upwards.

Hold your cube like this:

Remember the colour in the centre –

this is your **FAVOURITE** colour.

This is the same sequence we used when we climbed through the boulder field in Chapter 2, but here we do it twice!

As you make your way back through the boulder field you go...

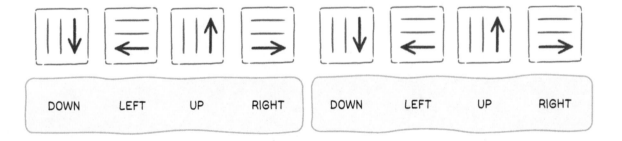

Is YELLOW facing upwards?

NO	YES

REPEAT

the sequence.

Keep your **FAVOURITE**
colour facing you.

Move another corner piece that
does **NOT** have yellow facing
upwards into this position...
by rotating the **TOP** layer.

REPEAT the sequence.

Don't worry that
the rest of the
cube is
MIXED UP

When **ALL 4 CORNERS** have YELLOW facing upwards, **ROTATE** the **TOP** layer to
solve the cube!

Now your cube looks
like this:

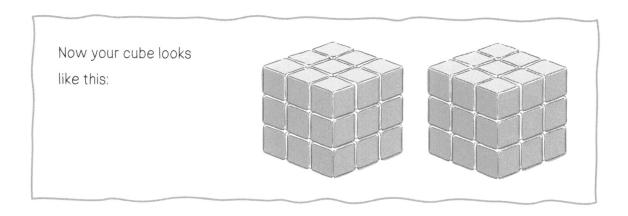

Great job!

Try to keep this story in mind as you practise the cube,
and in time you will be able to solve it without opening
this book!

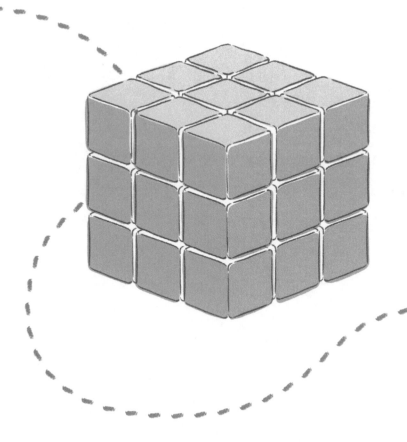

PART 4

PRACTISING THE SEQUENCES

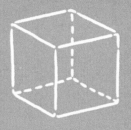

Practise makes perfect!

In Part 4 of this book, we will focus on
practising and memorising the sequences that
we use to solve the cube.

You can practise these sequences with your
cube **IN ANY PATTERN** – we're just learning
the moves and creating "muscle memory".

CHAPTER 1

You found a treasure map!

| LOOK **DOWN** AT YOUR MAP | **OPEN** YOUR MAP | **CIRCLE** THE WHITE CROSS | **CLOSE** YOUR MAP |

CHAPTER 2

As you clamber over the boulders, you go...

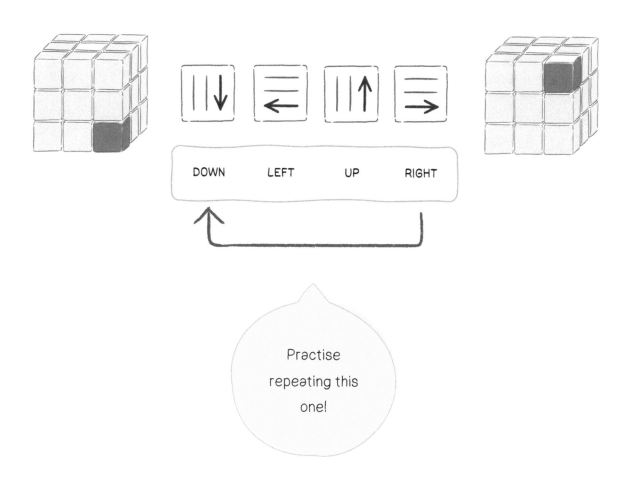

DOWN   LEFT   UP   RIGHT

Practise repeating this one!

CHAPTER 3

Sequence

Time to catch a fish!

STEP **AWAY** FROM THE HOLE	FISH JUMPS **UP**	TRY TO **CATCH** IT!	FISH JUMPS **DOWN**

STEP **TOWARDS** THE HOLE	FISH **CIRCLES TOWARDS** YOU	STEP **AWAY**	FISH **CIRCLES AWAY** FROM YOU

CHAPTER 3

Sequence **B**

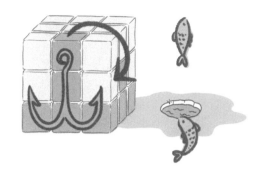

Time to catch a fish!

STEP **AWAY** FROM THE HOLE	FISH JUMPS **UP**	TRY TO **CATCH** IT!	FISH JUMPS **DOWN**

STEP **TOWARDS** THE HOLE	FISH **CIRCLES TOWARDS** YOU	STEP **AWAY**	FISH **CIRCLES AWAY** FROM YOU

This sequence is a mirror image of sequence **A** but the words are the same!

CHAPTER 4

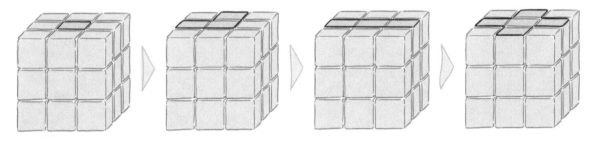

Let's use the balloon to get a better view and find the
yellow cross...

| ROLL INTO THE BALLOON | FLOAT UP | HEAD WIND | FLOAT DOWN | TAIL WIND | ROLL OUT OF THE BALLOON |

CHAPTER 5

Time to head home via the river...

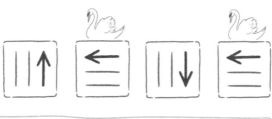

| ROW UP THE RIVER | 1 SWAN SWIMS PAST | ROW DOWN THE RIVER | 1 SWAN SWIMS PAST |

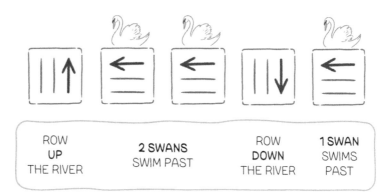

| ROW UP THE RIVER | 2 SWANS SWIM PAST | ROW DOWN THE RIVER | 1 SWAN SWIMS PAST |

CHAPTER 6

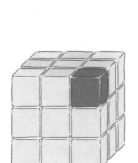

There is a storm coming...

| WIND FROM THE **FRONT** | SAILS **UP** AT THE FRONT | WIND FROM THE **BACK** | SAILS **UP** AT THE BACK | | WIND FROM THE **FRONT** | SAILS **DOWN** AT THE FRONT | WIND FROM THE **BACK** | SAILS **DOWN** AT THE BACK |

Practise repeating this one!

CHAPTER 7

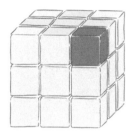

As you clamber over the boulders, you go...

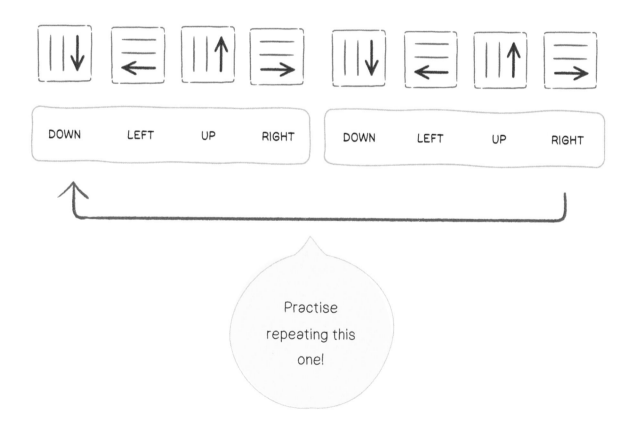

DOWN   LEFT   UP   RIGHT

DOWN   LEFT   UP   RIGHT

Practise repeating this one!

Impressive stuff!

Solving the cube is a huge achievement...
memorising it is an even bigger one.

Take your time, keep trying and, most importantly,
keep having fun.

Made in the USA
Middletown, DE
15 October 2023

40847139R10062